Then & **Now**
CRAWLEY

Then & Now
CRAWLEY

ROGER BASTABLE

TEMPUS

*This book is dedicated to my
Old Crawley family and my New Crawley friends,
but especially to my mother Janet and late father Peter
who belong to both categories.*

First published 2004

Tempus Publishing Limited
The Mill, Brimscombe Port,
Stroud, Gloucestershire, GL5 2QG
www.tempus-publishing.com

British Library Cataloguing in Publication Data.
A catalogue record for this book is available from the British Library.

ISBN 0 7524 3063 7

Typesetting and origination by Tempus Publishing Limited
Printed in Great Britain by Midway Colour Print, Wiltshire

CONTENTS

ACKNOWLEDGEMENTS

Having drawn from photographs of Crawley I have gathered over the past twenty or more years, and with some having become almost 'common currency', it is difficult to acknowledge individual photographs. I would, therefore, prefer to acknowledge those very kind and helpful people who have helped me in building up my 'Then' collection since 1980 and those who have allowed me to take photographs for the 'Now' section. In no particular order they include: Charles Kay of Crawley Library, Peter Gwynne, Peter Allen, Ian Hill, Evelyn Masse, the late Sir Norman Longley, Rod Balkham, Margaret Butler, Margaret Borrer, staff from the Crawley New Towns Commission, Peter Wickert, Headteacher of The Holy Trinity School, the Revd Malcolm Liles (Rector of Crawley), the Clergy of the Friary Church of SS Francis and Anthony, the proprietors of the Crawley Leisure Park, the editor of the *Crawley Observer*, Mr Camfield, the late Mrs Walpole, Mr Ivan Hill, Jim and Edna Briggs, the late Les Collins and the Crawley Museum Society which continues to do sterling work in preserving and recording the town's past. I am conscious that I have left out an equally long list of names and apologise, again thanking all those who are anxious to keep Crawley's long and colourful history alive by giving or loaning me photographs and postcards. All the 'Now' photographs were taken by me. I would also like to thank those who have helped me in other ways in producing this book, including Justin Wheelhouse who has patiently taught me the rudiments of computer technology, Matilda Pearce and the staff of Tempus Publishing, Martin Hayes from West Sussex County Archives who originally suggested that I compile this book, and my friend and fellow writer, Jeff Gardiner who read the proofs and whose excellent grasp of the intricacies of the English language rescued me from many a grammatical gaffe!

INTRODUCTION

Crawley's history is unusual in as much as it covers two towns rather than one. Although like countless villages, towns and cities it originated in the early Middle Ages (its name derives from *crow lea*, Old English for 'forest clearing with crows'), Crawley has the more recent distinction of being designated one of Britain's first post-war New Towns in 1947. The contrast between these two merits could not be more marked, with Crawley's two towns providing excellent examples of town development over seven centuries.

From the consecration of St. John's Church as the medieval chantry chapel in the mid-thirteenth century to its New Town designation in the middle of the twentieth, Crawley evolved and grew around its High Street with St. John's at its heart. No form of co-ordinated planning existed at this time, so even today evidence can be found of architecture spanning seven centuries, with the 1250 St. John's Church and the 2003 Asda Superstore barely a stone's throw apart. It is only relatively recently that Crawley High Street's development has been monitored, with its designation by the Borough Council in 1986 as an Historical Conservation Area.

In sharp contrast, Crawley New Town was planned to the last detail. Anthony Minoprio's Master Plan of 1948 was drawn up according to specific 'zones', with areas set aside for industry, residential neighbourhoods and the New Town shopping precinct. Just as the old town had focused on the High Street, this proposed urban utopia was centred around the spacious Queens Square. The designation and planning of Crawley, along with Stevenage, Harlow, Hatfield, Hemel Hempstead, Basildon, Bracknell and Welwyn Garden City, came as a direct result of the publication in 1898 of Ebenezer Howard's *Tomorrow: A Peaceful Path to Real Reform,* reprinted in 1902 as *Garden Cities of Tomorrow.* Although only one of a succession of utopians in search of the ideal urban community, Howard's ideals actually led to reality with the formation of the Garden Cities Association in 1899, resulting in the building of Letchworth (1903) and Welwyn (1919) Garden Cities. It was Howard's legacy which prompted governments to formulate the town planning scheme of which Crawley New Town was an early pioneer.

While considering the various ways of planning this compilation, it appeared that the most appropriate approach was to follow Crawley's development over seven centuries. Consequently it is divided into two parts; Crawley Old Town and Crawley New Town. The first was an informal arrangement centred around the High Street, and the 'Then' photographs in this section date from the mid-nineteenth to the mid-twentieth centuries. Its pattern runs from north to south, and is based on the Old Crawley quip that its High Street was the longest in the universe – from The Sun to The Half Moon public houses. Although areas of Crawley High Street were never formally named, I have identified them by their popular names of Northgate, Crawley Green, The Square and The Railway. The second part of the book, dealing with Crawley New Town, is more appropriately sequenced, following as it does the 1948 Master Plan. That this second part is shorter is not to underestimate its importance, but rather to reflect that the New Town is still a relatively recent chapter in Crawley's history.

What each of the two parts of the book have in common is the 'Then and Now' format. Despite their excellent motives and intentions, the New Town planners could not really predict the future and the original target of 50,000 inhabitants has doubled since the projected 'cut off' year of 1963. One thing underestimated by the planners was the number of cars and parking facilities that would be needed in the neighbourhoods and town centre.

Finally, as an environmental consolation for the unpredicted volume of cars in the town, photographing Old and New Crawley in the present day has shown how much greener the town has become in terms of trees and shrubs.

Apart from its historical interest, I hope that one positive outcome of this compilation is the evidence that, for Crawley, environmental awareness and urbanisation have become as compatible as Ebenezer Howard would have wished. As someone born of an Old Crawley family the same year that the New Town was formally inaugurated, I am among the first to appreciate and cherish its long history as conserved in the High Street and other parts of the area. However, I do not empathise with those who bemoan the present New Town. In any case, pre-1950 memories of Crawley as a 'sleepy little village' are largely mythical, since this aspect of the town had disappeared soon after the arrival of the railway a century before. With its prime position, it is highly likely that Crawley would have been developed further after 1945, and, despite certain mistakes made in planning, its designation as a New Town controlled this inevitable growth. My final, and fondest, hope is that those who read this book will be equally proud of Crawley's present as its past, and optimistic for its future.

Chapter 1

OLD CRAWLEY

Because of its concentration on detail, this map of Crawley High Street in the 1870s is almost pictorial with its inclusion of trees and labelling of public buildings. It also shows that, even 130 years ago, Crawley had ceased to be a village and was well on the way to becoming a small town. Virtually nothing about the High Street as seen on this map was planned. Nonetheless a specific pattern of urban growth had evolved around its central thoroughfare, which almost exactly marked the half-way point on the main London to Brighton road.

During the eighteenth and early nineteenth centuries, local trade revolved around The George, The White Hart and The Rising Sun coaching inns. The coming of the railway to Crawley in 1848 resulted in expansion, not only in the High Street, but also to the west and south with the development by speculative builders of West Green and Southgate (identified here as 'New Town'). One of the most interesting parts of this Victorian Crawley New Town development is what was marked on this map as Church Road and later as Robinson Road. At the turn of the century it housed two chapels, the local school, cottage hospital and post office. By 2003 it had entirely disappeared under the Asda Superstore development.

An Old Crawley quip was that it boasted the longest High Street in the universe since it stretched from The Sun to The Half Moon public houses!

The first chapter on Old Crawley will take the reader on this long walk from The Sun on the High Street's northern boundary to The Half Moon, which is to the south of the railway line.

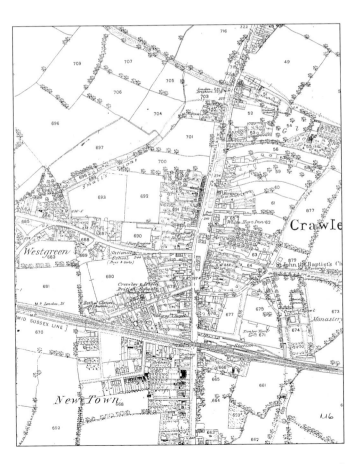

T he first photograph dates from around 1903 and shows the High Street's northern boundary where it met the London road. To the left stands The Sun Inn, while to the right are Albert Cottages, presumably named after Queen Victoria's husband. At the Great Exhibition of 1851, Albert took a particular interest in what were patronisingly known as 'model houses for the labouring classes' at Kennington, and it was appropriate that these cottages were named after him when they were built around the 1880s. This view of Crawley High Street would have been instantly recognisable until the 1980s with the cottages' demolition.

The same view today shows that nothing remains. A smart office development which now dominates this part of Crawley replaced Albert Cottages in the 1980s, while The Sun Inn was demolished about ten years later as part of the Crawley Leisure Park development. Brannigans, which specialises in 'dancing and cavorting', has replaced The Sun Inn, and while many of Crawley's older residents might despise what stands here now, Brannigans perfectly symbolises popular leisure in 2003, just as The Sun Inn did a century before.

Towards the end of the 1940s the fields alongside The Sun became the home of Crawley Town Football Club. Here it remained for fifty years, and, as football played a significant part in Crawley's culture in the years after the Second World War, it was an appropriate predecessor for Crawley Leisure Park. The photograph below shows the opening of the new south stand in around 1953. To the far right of the stand with his wife Kath and daughter Angela is Jack Norman, who at the age of ninety remains an enthusiastic supporter of the Crawley 'Reds'. After the removal of Crawley Town Football Club to Broadfield Stadium in 1997 and the development of the area where the south stand once stood, this site is now a corner of Crawley Leisure Park's car park with Ifield Avenue, one of the New Town's link roads, behind.

Youngmans and Crawley Town teams shortly before kick-off. Youngmans was the first company from south London to relocate to the New Town and this match was one of the first occasions when Old and New Crawley met. Youngmans' captain, Fred Kennard, went on to become one of Crawley Town's first New Town players and is still a keen supporter over fifty years later. My father Peter and his brothers played for Crawley Town in the late 1940s and early 1950s, and on this occasion Doug and Philip Bastable are in the Crawley team's pre-match line-up. When Crawley Town moved to Broadfield Stadium at Southgate in 1997, the site was redeveloped as Crawley Leisure Park, with facilities (undreamed of in 1949) including a multi-screen cinema, ten-pin bowling, fitness centre and leading restaurants.

Crawley Town's ground at Town Meadow behind The Sun Inn was laid out around the same time as plans were being drawn up for Crawley New Town, and this team photograph is a reminder of both. Dating from 3 December 1949, it shows the

In the early years of the twentieth century, fields behind Albert Cottages were the home of Crawley Cricket Club – the rather formal photograph below of the local team dates from 1911. In contrast, the photograph of the Crawley 'Ramblers' Cricket Club (right) is very relaxed and dates from about 1950. Based at The White Hart in Crawley High Street, the Ramblers team was made up of New Towners such as Fred Kennard and local characters such as Philip Bastable, Tommy Regan, Ken Cheesman, Les Hall, Tommy Foster and the inimitable 'Shiner' Wilson.

However, the gatekeeper's cottage still stood, with the name 'Crawley' crudely painted on a white-washed background along its north-facing wall. Crawley's toll gate keepers were great characters, some by all accounts not above a little bribery. Just below the painted name of Crawley there would probably have been a Board of Tolls, usually ranging from a few pence to a few shillings, depending on the size of vehicle and number of wheels. The same view today shows an equally busy part of Crawley High Street with the northern end of the High Street relief road filtering in towards the London road. The 1900s view shows a very tranquil scene, but it is likely that during the 'golden age of coaching' a century before, this part of the High Street would have been as teeming with traffic as it is today.

The name 'Northgate' derives from the North toll gate which stood at the northern boundary of the Crawley Turnpike. By the time of this old photograph in the early 1900s, the actual toll gate, which closed the road and only opened upon payment of a toll, had long since gone.

Although it only had a population of a few hundred until the middle of the nineteenth century, the village of Crawley would have been teeming with life in the 1830s when coaches called hourly during the day. Marking half way on the London to Brighton road, Crawley was a convenient venue for a break in the journey and the changing of horses. Unsurprisingly, the village boasted three large coaching inns; once travellers passed the North toll gate, they would find the first, The Rising Sun, on the eastern side of the street. According to the 1839 Directory, The Rising Sun was a commercial and posting inn with Mr James Newman as innkeeper. There is little doubt that, like most coaching inns of the time, The Rising Sun was a boisterous place with dealings in smuggled goods at times, but there is little evidence here. Dating from the early 1900s, the photograph below shows Crawley's coaching days long since gone and records the building's more sedate identity as shops and a small private school run by Mr John Conlan. Nonetheless, the Regency influence is still evident from the bay windows. As was common with other properties in the High Street, the demolition of relatively recent buildings revealed a much older structure beneath.

The same view today shows that this somewhat bland end of Crawley High Street now has little to remind us of its more animated past. One saving grace is that the 1980s office developments are varied, with an attempt to emulate the tile-hanging which was a particular feature of old Northgate buildings.

A favourite photograph of old Northgate, which, as well as giving a close-up of the pair of tiny cottages known today as Boscobel, also captures a clear image of what was literally a 'cottage industry'. Standing alongside The Rising Sun, the cottage was a timber-framed structure, faced with tiles on the upper part of the building.

The photograph also shows the inhabitants, Mr and Mrs Chart (and cat). Mr Chart stands alongside his tricycle, showing that he was Crawley's billposter. Fresh from his printing works behind, Mr Chart can be imagined cycling around the area delivering posters for local sales, exhibitions, fêtes and sporting events. His 'patch' was evidently wide, since the posters fixed to the cottage fence advertise events as far away as Ifield, Worth and even Mannings Heath, near Horsham. Although the posters have dates, it is difficult to decipher them, but the photograph probably dates from around 1902. The same view today not only shows a greatly restored building, but a reminder of just how small cottages like the Charts' were. As an office almost certainly with computers and fax machines, Boscobel could almost be regarded as a cottage industry – 2003 style.

In grander contrast to Boscobel and a little further along the High Street stood The Tree. The Tree was a much older, timber-framed building than its brick exterior would suggest. In the early Middle Ages it was Crawley's manor house, and the Moot Hall behind it (latterly known as the Crawley Barn) was dismantled in 1970 to be reconstructed at the Weald and Downland Open Air Museum at Singleton. By the time it was photographed around the 1880s, the house was occupied by the Smith family. Dr Thomas Smith was Crawley's leading physician from the late 1820s until his death in 1862. John Leech, who went on to illustrate *Punch* and some of Charles Dickens' early novels, lived here briefly in the 1830s as a medical student. Just as famous as The Tree was the Crawley Elm after which it was named, the remains of which can be seen in front of the house. Reputedly many hundreds of years old by this time, the Crawley Elm was little more than a stump, but so broad that a

small room was created from it, complete with door and gate. To the right of the photograph are the gates to Crawley Rectory and in the foreground is the Green from which this part of Crawley High Street got its name. Although the remains of the Crawley Elm vanished many years ago, the same view of the house (above) shows it to be little changed, despite its modern metal window frames. The house is now owned by Crawley Borough Council and is the premises of the Crawley Council for Voluntary Service (CCVS).

very high prices on the open market. This is an early photograph of Crawley Rectory, dating from the late 1860s or early 1870s, when occupied by the Revd John Soper BA, Rector from 1855 to 1876. The house was surrounded by well-manicured gardens and a paddock in which garden parties, fêtes and bazaars would be held. Crawley Rectory was demolished in the late 1950s in favour of (slightly) more modest modern premises alongside St John's Church. The land where Crawley's Victorian rectory had stood was developed in 1963 with the construction of what then was the Woodall-Duckham office block. As the more recent photograph shows, the site has changed beyond all recognition, and will do still further if plans to redevelop the northern perimeter of the town centre go ahead. The original drive and accompanying land of Crawley Rectory was opened up in the mid-1950s for The Boulevard.

After the landed gentry, the second rung of Victorian Crawley's social ladder was occupied by the rector of the parish, whose residence on Crawley Green reflected his status. Crawley Rectory was by far the grandest house in the High Street, with a long drive and its own lodge alongside The Tree. Built around the 1840s, Crawley Rectory was designed in distinctive early-Victorian 'ecclesiastical' style; examples can still be found in the West Country and fetch

A striking contrast to Crawley Rectory is The Punch Bowle, which shows little sign of change even in the fifty years that separate these two photographs. The Punch Bowle was almost certainly built in the fifteenth century and is a fine example of a Sussex Wealden house. The exterior was restored in the 1920s to give some idea of how the original house, probably the home of a prosperous yeoman farmer, might have looked. Although we have some idea of its original appearance and of its more recent history, the centuries in between are something of a closed book. By the early years of the twentieth century it was a dilapidated pair of cottages. The revival of road traffic after the First World War led to extensive restoration and renovation when the building became The Punch Bowle Tea Shop, enjoying thriving business in the 1920s and '30s due to motor traffic from London to Brighton. For forty years the building was a branch first of the National Provincial and then of the National Westminster Bank. The name Punch Bowle was re-adopted by brewers Greene King when it was opened as a pub in the early 1990s. In the older photograph, dating from around 1947, a couple of schoolboys are taking part in what appears to be a survey of the town at the time of its New Town designation. These were to be Old Crawley's final years; Crawley Rectory was still occupied by the Revd D.L. Couper, and the Rectory Lodge is to the left of the photograph. Despite changes in The Punch Bowle's immediate vicinity, the 2003 photograph shows the building little changed, with just a glimpse of The Boulevard in the distance.

These photographs illustrate how varied the architectural styles and dates of Crawley High Street were – and still are – with the Embassy cinema, opened in 1938, directly opposite The Punch Bowle, which dates from five centuries earlier. The Embassy is a fine example of inter-war cinema architecture and was the centre of Crawley's popular cultural life for well over thirty years, when 'going to the pictures' was the highlight of the week for all ages. Once a week, on Saturday morning, the Embassy was taken over by schoolchildren for its weekly matinées, with seats priced at a shilling, nine pence and sixpence when I went there in the late 1950s and early 1960s. That the circle was out of bounds was hardly surprising. The weekly programme was usually made up of old black and white cowboy films and serials such as the original 1940s version of *Batman and Robin*. Once the morning's programme was over there would be a rush for Mrs Fielder's sweet shop (now KFC) alongside Doreen's Café. In its heyday of the 1950s and 1960s, the evening queue would often encircle the building. It was converted to a three-screen cinema in 1980 and finally closed in the late 1990s. Little has changed of the buildings in the fifty or more years which separate these photographs, although their occupancy reflects a very different age. Doreen's Café is now the Fortune Villa Chinese restaurant, while the Embassy has been converted into Bar Med, a favourite nightspot for Crawley's youth.

These cottages on Crawley Green were probably never given a specific name. The bottom photograph dates from around 1964 and shows a board advertising that the site was to become the premises for Tesco, the modern supermarket that opened here in late 1965 after all the cottages were demolished. Like The Tree (which has mercifully survived), these cottages were much older than their brick and tile-hung exterior would suggest. Cottages such as these were in profusion on Crawley Green up to the 1930s; sadly none survive today. The photograph (right) showing the same view today indicates that so much of 1960s architecture failed to complement what had stood before. What was the Tesco supermarket from 1965 to 1968 later became the Green Shield Stamp shop and later still Argos.

Today it is the premises for The Rat and Parrot public house. An attempt to 'Victorianise' made an ugly building look even worse, especially as some 1960s buildings in the town have been revitalised. One redeeming feature is that the area is now bedecked with more trees and shrubs than it was forty years ago.

In comparison to The Square further along the High Street, Crawley Green has suffered badly from developments over the past sixty years or more. The first photograph, dating from around 1905, shows the distinctive character of Crawley Green as it must have been for centuries, with its blend of tile-hung cottages and timber-framed houses on either side. No buildings which stood there a century ago have survived. Not only this, but little (if any) effort was made to replace them with anything distinctive. The blame for this cannot be laid entirely at the door of the New Town developers, since a fine row of houses, some of which dated back hundreds of years, was demolished in the mid-1930s to make way for Grand Parade. One encouraging feature of these two photographs, taken almost a century apart, is the retention of Crawley Green and the growth of its trees. Since the Jubilee Oak that marked Queen Victoria's Golden Jubilee in 1887, the Green has been planted with many commemorative trees, such as the 1897 Diamond Jubilee Oak between Boscobel and The Tree. More recent additions include a Canadian Maple tree planted by Princess Elizabeth in January 1950 to commemorate Canadian forces stationed in the area during the Second World War.

This charming pair of cottages with bow-fronted windows look as though it might have stepped straight out of a Jane Austen novel. Dating from the early nineteenth century, its distinctive Regency style is a reminder of the days when the Prince Regent would pass through Crawley en route to his magnificent Royal Pavilion in Brighton. Although this style still predominates in the Prince's favourite South Coast resort, sadly it was the only one of its kind in Crawley High Street. By the time it was photographed sometime in the 1870s, the front parlour of the right-hand cottage was converted into one of Crawley's first shops, Mr Horatio Mitchell's general stores. Apart from the building's design and attractiveness, unique in Crawley, this photograph is an interesting record of how the High Street's first shops emerged by doing business from the front parlour. As far as I am aware the cottages had no name, but were known within Old Crawley as Camfield's the Tailors after Mr Camfield who ran his little shop here during the middle years of the twentieth century. The shop appeared much the same until its demolition in around 1965. A 1980s office development now stands on the site.

Neighbouring Camfield's the Tailors to the north were the much older Rose Cottages, probably dating from the Middle Ages. As with Camfield's, this is a fascinating photograph not just of architecture, but of Old Crawley life, since it is a snapshot showing excited residents decking out their cottages with bunting to celebrate the Silver Jubilee of King George V in May 1935. Once again there is an example of tile-hanging, which was a common feature of Northgate and Crawley Green. When Rose Cottages were sadly demolished in the early 1950s, the tile-hanging and interior partitions were stripped away to reveal a fine timber-framed structure which showed signs of them possibly being part of a medieval long hall. Barclays Bank now stands on the site.

This photograph (below), taken from The Square, shows Crawley Green almost in its entirety as it would have appeared about a century ago. This is a view which has probably changed little in 200 years or more. None of the buildings to the left of the photograph, which include Camfields and Rose Cottages, now survive, but those to the right still exist. Another interesting aspect of this photograph is that it gives a clear perspective of the Green itself, which was probably once entirely open and clear of trees. The first of the Green's commemorative trees, the Jubilee Oak planted in 1887 and seen here to the right, is still very young compared with the same view today, where it dominates this part of the High Street. Since photography was invented at more or less the same time as the coming of the railway, even Crawley's earliest photographs give no indication of the bustle and activity generated by the horse-drawn coaches which passed through on the hour at the beginning of Queen Victoria's reign. Many of the old cottages on the western side of Crawley Green were demolished in the mid-1930s for the appropriately named Grand Parade, purpose-built shops designed to the popular neo-Georgian 'Home Counties' style of architecture. The first major retail shop to occupy Grand Parade was Woolworths, whose central position is now the premises of The Jubilee Oak public house.

This gives a closer view of the south-eastern part of Crawley Green just off the picture in the previous photograph of Old Crawley. Dating from around 1953, it shows a row of cottages similar to Rose Cottages, boarded up ready for demolition in preparation for the construction of The Broadwalk and first phase of the New Town Shopping Centre. In the first half of the twentieth century at least three of these tiny cottages were also small business premises. To the left was Miss Heathfield's sweet shop, while a couple of doors further along was her sister-in-law's tea shop, next to Mr Corke's shoe repairers. As the demolition of these cottages was part of Crawley Development Corporation's New Town Shopping Centre scheme, Mr and Mrs Heathfield were re-housed in a modern maisonette in the new West Green neighbourhood. Despite the modern facilities of their new home, the Heathfields greatly missed the little cottage where they had lived, worked and brought up their family for many years. With the benefit of hindsight, this area might have been more attractive if restored and renovated in the style of The Causeway in Horsham, with The Broadwalk located further along the High Street. Yet the climate of the time, with its emphasis on contemporary architecture, produced little outcry over the demolition of buildings that were hundreds of years old. The Jubilee Oak (which was mercifully spared) is now such a size that its is difficult to compare the same view today. The only building to survive is The Brewery Shades (now simply Shades) public house.

This old view of The White Hart public house dates from around the 1870s. The White Hart would have been the second of Crawley's coaching inns to welcome travel-worn passengers from London in the early years of the nineteenth century. That it was one of the best equipped, with a blacksmith and extensive stabling behind, was probably due to the fact that it was the home of Crawley's first post office in 1810 with The White Hart's innkeeper, James Swift, its first postmaster. In 1828 Crawley's first full-time postmaster, William Mitchell (brother of Horatio) was sworn in, with the house alongside the inn as the first post office. As was the custom, even the post office became a 'family concern', with William's son Charles succeeding him. It stayed within the Mitchell family until Charles retired in 1908. This early photograph suggests that The White Hart was made up of two buildings, with the right-hand part clearly the older due to its Horsham-stone roof. The rails for tethering horses at the front were still in place in the 1950s. Facing both the Jubilee Oak and the wider, central part of the High Street known as The Square, The White Hart has changed surprisingly little in the intervening century and a quarter. Unlike some, The White Hart still enjoys the reputation of an old-fashioned public house, thus happily retaining its character both inside and out. With the return of the High Street market in the late 1990s (below), The White Hart again looks out over a familiar part of Old Crawley.

A nother of the many buildings to have a Horsham-stone roof was The Bay Tree Coffee House, directly opposite The White Hart, on the western side of The Square. As with part of The White Hart, The Bay Tree's roof is an indication that the building was older than its sash windows and clapboard facing suggest. In much the same way as Crawley High Street has today become a focus for restaurants and wine bars, so a century or more ago was it the home of many coffee and tea shops. Dating from around the 1880s, this fascinating old photograph tells us that the proprietor, Mr Ambrose Shaw, was evidently something of a late-Victorian entrepreneur. As well being a coffee house proprietor, Mr Shaw also specialised in the repair of bicycles and sewing machines. Two fascinating details are the penny-farthings and the gas lamp. As the years went by the mechanical side of the business grew, so that by the early years of the twentieth century a motorcycle shop was built on the front garden. In common with other local tradesmen, Shaw's became very respected and synonymous with car sales and repairs which expanded to the rear of The Bay Tree. Later becoming Jones the greengrocers and then a handicraft shop, the building was demolished in the 1980s. It was replaced by 'Si' (formerly 'La Strada') Italian restaurant, a modern building which complements the High Street's older architecture. The left-hand part of the Bay Tree was demolished and replaced by an extension to The George Hotel in around 1902

Apart from Gatwick Airport, Crawley's best known building has to be The George Hotel at the very centre of The Square on the High Street, a lasting reminder of the town's eighteenth and early nineteenth-century claim to fame as the half-way mark on the London to Brighton road. One of the best evocations of The George Inn as it was then can be found in Sir Arthur Conan-Doyle's novel *Rodney Stone* (1896): 'And then at last, we saw the formless mass of the huge Crawley elm looming before us in the gloom, and there was the broad village street with the glimmer of the cottage windows, and the high front of the old George Inn, glowing from every door and pane and crevice, in honour of the noble company who were to sleep within that night.' Despite its reputation as one of Britain's best known coaching inns, The George is far older than can be seen from this photograph which dates from around 1870. Although first mentioned in the 1580 will of Richard Covert, much of the building seen here

is older still, as is suggested by its Horsham-stone roof. Its timber-framed structure was all but hidden by nineteenth-century tile-hanging and plasterwork, but this is probably how The George would have looked in its Regency heyday. It was not until 1902 that the building was extended northwards, and it was during the 1930s that it was given its distinctive ground-floor façade shown in the recent photograph. In more recent years the hotel has worked hard to preserve both The George's and Old Crawley's heritage.

The George Hotel has made such a major contribution to Crawley's identity and architecture that it is destined to make more than one appearance in any photographic compilation of the area. The top photograph, dating from 1903, shows the building in the middle of The Square known as the George Annexe. As its name would suggest, the Annexe was built around the beginning of the nineteenth century to house the overflow of guests from The George Inn itself. It is worth noting that, as the inn sign hanging from the gallows across the street testifies, the hotel's name derives from St George rather than the Prince Regent who was reputedly a regular visitor en route to Brighton. The young Queen Victoria was alleged to make a brief stop at The George in 1837 on a visit to the Royal Pavilion which she had recently inherited. Unhappily for Crawley, and even more so for Brighton, Victoria took a strong dislike to her uncle's ornate residence and ultimately sold it to Brighton Corporation in 1850. Although no royal visitor appears to have stayed there since, Queen Elizabeth II has visited The George twice, for tea during her visit in January 1950 and for lunch in June 1958. Apart from the Annexe, which was demolished in 1934, this panoramic view of The Square looking north has changed relatively little in the hundred years which separate these two photographs, due mainly to the High Street's recent pedestrianisation.

Immediately opposite The George and on the other side of the Annexe (to the left of the photograph) stands a building which has had many functions and almost as many names over the years, but which is still generally known as The Ancient Priors. A twin-gabled house which probably dates from the mid-fifteenth century, The Ancient Priors, along with The Punch Bowle, is the best example in Crawley High Street of a timber-framed house restored to look much as it did when first built. At the beginning of the twentieth century it was known as The Priest's House, since it was likely that it was a medieval religious house attached to the chantry chapel which is now St John's Parish Church. Like many buildings of its age, The Ancient Priors has lived through changing fortunes, possibly being used as a priest's house, private residence, tenement housing and the original White Hart Inn in the eighteenth century. At the time of this photograph (bottom) around 100 years ago, most of the ground floor was made over to Mr Burgess's furniture shop. The Ancient Priors entered a more genteel phase in the 1920s when the original timbers were exposed and restored and it became an antique shop, tea shop and restaurant. Today it is a branch of Ask Italian restaurants.

The first of these four photographs illustrating change in Crawley High Street shows the junction between Ifield Road and the High Street and dates from the early 1900s. The seventeenth-century (or earlier) premises of Nathaniel Miller's saddler's shop is a building which contributed a great deal to the variety of architecture in Crawley High Street. Miller's was one of a number of buildings with a Horsham-stone roof which disguised an older structure than its plaster facing and sash windows would suggest. Miller's was owned by one of Crawley's oldest trading families and even more fascinating than the building is the probable figure of Nathaniel Miller himself standing outside his shop, which is hung with leather saddles beneath the horse's head, the traditional symbol of his trade. The second photograph shows the same scene about thirty years later when the shop front has been slightly modernised. Not long after it was

photographed, Miller's was demolished, responsibility for which cannot be laid at the New Town's door since it was carried out in the mid-1930s. Miller's was replaced by the cold uniformity of a branch of Barclays Bank with Flynn's the dry cleaners and a ladies' milliners alongside. A second storey was added in around 1964 and the building is now occupied by a branch of The Royal Bank of Scotland.

While it is interesting to look at Crawley High Street's individual buildings over time and hear the stories each has to tell, more general views are sometimes necessary in order to gain an overall perspective. This is a favourite old photograph of the High Street (top), dating from around 1870. Looking south, with Ifield Road Corner to the right and what today is known as Church Walk to the left, the photograph lends support to the theory that Crawley's original thoroughfare was not the London to Brighton road, but rather the east-west route which linked the medieval parishes of Worth and Ifield with the larger market towns of East Grinstead and Horsham. The theory is backed up by the tiny cottage in the middle of The Square, complete with front garden and fence, which stood on this east-west route. Compared to the 2003 photograph, the eastern side of The Square seems very much intact apart from the demolition in 1898 of a tiny row of cottages to provide a High Street approach to St John's Parish Church. In 1870 the only access to the church, including weddings and funerals, was via Church Walk. The western side, however, has greatly altered, the only buildings to survive the past 130 years being the timber-framed house to the right (again concealed behind plasterwork and sash windows) and the tall, red-brick house which in 1870 would have been The Morning Star Inn. By 2003 both are dwarfed by a brick office block built in 1988.

For most villages and towns, the most historically significant building is the parish church, where the whole community would meet for the festivals of Christmas, Easter and Harvest, and where families would gather for baptisms, marriages and funerals. Founded as a small chantry chapel in 1250, Crawley's parish church, dedicated to St John the Baptist, grew in three distinct stages. The second came around the middle of the fifteenth century with the addition of the tower and the raising of the nave under its fine oak roof. With various alterations in between, the third phase in St John's growth came in the 1880s with an extensive programme of external and internal changes brought about by the Revd John Barrett-Lennard, Rector from 1876 to 1898. This old photograph looking west from St John's dates from around the 1860s, before Barrett-

Lennard's ambitious building programme which involved the rebuilding and enlarging of the chancel. Other than the extension of the chancel, the 2003 view does not vary greatly from that of a century and a quarter before. The other addition is the placing of a clock on each side of the tower to commemorate the life and reign of Queen Victoria, erected in the year of her death in 1901.

These photographs of the interior of St John's Church date from almost exactly the same period as the previous exterior ones. The first, which dates from the 1860s or '70s, shows the building before the addition of the north aisle and the rebuilding of the chancel by Barrett-Lennard in the early 1880s. Suspicious of the resurgence of Roman Catholicism, the Victorian Church of England tended to emphasise its Protestantism as can be seen by the Ten Commandments set in stone plaques either side of the altar. Public worship was certainly more casual than it is today, as we learn from the diaries of the Victorian hymn writer John Mason Neale, Rector of Crawley for a short time in 1842, who deplored the fact that the churchwarden once stood on the altar during a Sunday service to open the window! Evident in both photographs are the seventeenth-century pulpit, the memorial plaque (on the right-hand wall) to churchwarden Thomas Smith, local physician and resident of The Tree on Crawley Green who died in 1862, but above all the magnificent fifteenth-century oak roof. Crawley has always enjoyed relative prosperity and in the fifteenth century this was demonstrated by the use of oak. Following the example of John Barrett-Lennard, recent alterations were carried out by Rectors Michael Goode (1983-'93) and Keith Richards (1993-7).

This red-bricked, late eighteenth-century building is one of the most distinguished and distinctive in The Square. It was built as a private town house-style residence for Mr Richard Hall in the 1770s, and as was common with Georgian architecture, was elegantly symmetrical and simple in design. Like so many other buildings in Crawley High Street, the house has had a chequered history over two and a quarter centuries. During the middle years of the nineteenth century the building was The Morning Star Inn. This photograph dates from the 1880s when part of the ground floor was converted into Mr Eli Yetman's butcher shop. By the 1890s, the ground floor was divided into two shops with separate living accommodation above, the ornate Victorian 'shop dividers' still in evidence in the 2003 photograph. Two other interesting features in the older photograph are Mr Terry's Tinsmiths and Gasfitters shed, where Charles Warren's shop was to stand a few years later. Today the house has been greatly restored, preserving historical features at the same time as making it suitable for a modern business premises. The arch was opened up again with the building of Warrens Ironmongery Stores in the 1890s and was access to the rear for around a 100 years. Recent refurbishment has since closed it up.

When Richard Hall's Georgian house was divided into two retail premises in the 1890s, Yetmans the butchers occupied one (No. 36 High Street) while the other (No. 34) became a fishmongers under the name of Sproston. In 1922, my great-grandfather Harry Bastable bought the business for my grandfather Albert. After the First World War, Harry retired as a Chislehurst fishmonger and went to live in Brighton, making sure that his three sons carried on the family trade in Chislehurst and Crawley. This old photograph dates from around 1925 and shows Harry on the left-hand side of the marble fish slab and Albert on the other, with the name Bastable & Son appropriately over both. As well as being a fishmonger, Albert Bastable was also a dealer in poultry and game, hence the appearance of rabbits and pheasants hanging above the fish on the slab. Following Harry's death in 1937 and the end of the Second World War eight years later, Albert's own three sons worked with their father in the business, an arrangement which lasted until Albert's death aged eighty-six in February 1986. He was proud to be Crawley's oldest tradesman and finally gave up working in his High Street shop only six weeks before he died. Although the nature of business at 34 High Street has greatly changed since that time (left), the character of the building has been preserved, thanks to the planning regulations now demanded of Crawley High Street as a Historical Conservation Area.

Through the arch alongside Bastables' fish shop and 'up the yard' as we used to call it, there stood for nearly fifty years one of Old (and later New) Crawley's best-loved institutions – Bastables' Fish and Chip Shop. Begun in the 1940s by my grandmother Violet in a tiny brick outhouse originally used for the smoking of herrings, it grew to become one of Crawley's first and most popular takeaways. Run from the early 1950s by my parents Peter and Janet and their sister-in-law Ethel, Bastables' Fish and Chip Shop became more than just a 'chippy', but a place for Old (and New) Towners to gather and catch up on local news and gossip. In the forty or more years that they served up countless packets of chips and thousands of portions of battered cod, plaice or huss, Peter, Janet and Ethel got to know their customers through two or more generations. The photograph below dates from September 1990, just days before the shop closed and shows Peter, Janet and Ethel looking understandably cheerful at the prospect of imminent retirement. For a few years

afterwards, after a change of ownership and management, it operated as a kebab house, but was demolished in the late 1990s for redevelopment. The 2003 photograph above shows Janet standing on the site of Bastables' Fish and Chip Shop as the remaining member of the 1990 workforce, following Peter's death in 1997 and Ethel's in 2001. Even today, thirteen years after the shop's closure, Janet still meets former customers who greet her as a long-lost friend.

Directly opposite Warren's Ironmongery Stores around a century ago was Harry Gravelys' bakers shop. Like so many of Crawley High Street's shops, Gravelys' was a family concern and very personal, as the proprietors were known and active in the town. Although the building itself was unremarkable, the personal aspect of the business is literally writ clear. Gravelys' was a good example of family High Street trading, with the shop, a bakery behind and living accommodation above. Later Hills' the bakers, the building was demolished in the 1950s when it became Johnsons' Furniture Shop. Today the site is occupied by one of the Iceland chain of frozen food stores.

This old photograph of the junction of Three Bridges Road and the High Street dates from either the end of 1956 or the beginning of 1957 since Smith Clothing Co. is advertising its imminent move to The Martletts in the New Town Shopping Centre. Three Bridges Road, or Worth Lane as it was originally known, was the main thoroughfare east as Ifield Road was west, and traditionally marked the southernmost boundary of Crawley Parish. Even more interesting is the building alongside, which for almost 100 years was the premises for John Penfold, Corn and Coal Merchant. Penfold's was one of the first of Crawley High Street's historic buildings to be restored rather than demolished. Although difficult to realise, it is the only building which survives today. What was once Worth Lane and then Three Bridges Road is now Haslett Avenue, named after Dame Caroline Haslett who was a member of the Crawley Development Corporation which planned the New Town.

This photograph (top) of The Square is one of the oldest I have seen. Probably dating from the 1860s, it is a fine panorama of the High Street looking north showing how it must have looked for much of the early to mid-nineteenth century. What in the previous photograph was John Penfold's shop is seen here almost a century earlier to the far right, where a shop front had been added beneath the left-hand bay of what had clearly been a private house. Equally interesting is the one-storey building alongside, with the very high-pitched Horsham-stone roof. With a board over the door, it was certainly some sort of business, although it is impossible to make out the wording, while on the other side is the tall outline of The Morning Star. In the middle stood the block often known simply as The Square, seen on p.34 from the opposite side at about the same time. Although a jumble of assorted buildings, The Square added to this perspective of the High Street which lost a good deal of its character when demolished in 1958. In the same view in 2003, Penfold's as a building survives, although in greatly changed form, while The Morning Star house that once towered over neighbouring cottages is now dwarfed between buildings of the late twentieth century. This modern photograph gives a far more favourable view of the High Street than one taken even ten years before. Since 1986 the Borough Council has worked hard to ensure the conservation of the area by caring for old buildings and carrying out new development within the High Street's historical character.

For convenience I have named this fourth and final area of the High Street 'The Railway' as, although few buildings had direct connection with it, this part of Crawley developed following the coming of the railway to the town in 1848. The second half of the nineteenth century not only witnessed the growth of technology in Britain, of which the railway was a significant manifestation, but also new movements in religion and the arts. Until the erection in 1858 of the Bethel Reformed Baptist Chapel in New Road (later Robinson Road), St John's Church was the only place of worship in Crawley, the Church of England being the only Christian denomination apart from the 1676 (Quaker) Friends Meeting House in Langley Lane. The restrictions placed upon non-Anglican denominations were lifted in the nineteenth century, most notably in the case of the Roman Catholic Church. An eminent convert to Roman Catholicism was the widowed Mrs Mary Blunt of Crabbet Park. After his mother's death, Francis donated land in Worth Lane and £2,000 for the building of a Roman Catholic Church and Franciscan Friary, consecrated in 1861. The old photograph dates from 1958 shortly before the church's demolition, with the recent photograph showing the new church that was consecrated the following year.

Acomparison of these two
photographs of the interior of
Crawley's Franciscan Friary sums up the
changes which have taken place within
the Roman Catholic Church over the
past forty years, especially with the
Second Vatican Council of 1962-5.

The first photograph of the Friary
dating from around 100 years ago,
shows the devotion given to statues and
paintings. To the far right lies the tomb
of Francis Scawen Blunt of Crabbet Park,
benefactor of the Friary, who died in
1872. His younger brother Wilfrid, who
inherited the family estates, carved
Francis' effigy over his tomb based on
sketches made at Francis' deathbed.
When the Friary church was rebuilt in
the late 1950s, Francis' tomb remained
intact. The Franciscan brotherhood
remained until around 1980 after which
the Friary buildings were demolished,
leaving the simpler design of the modern
church with the altar unusually facing
south rather than east. Francis Blunt's
effigy has recently been restored and now
lies on the eastern side of the church.
The Friary churchyard houses the graves
of assorted characters such as the famous
nineteenth-century courtesan (and
Wilfrid Scawen Blunt's mistress),
Catherine 'Skittles' Walters and Lord
Alfred Douglas (friend of Oscar Wilde)

This happy picnic scene was taken around 1930 in what today are the Memorial Gardens, but known then as Crawley Recreation Ground or 'the Rec'. To the left is my grandmother Violet Bastable with her three young sons Doug, Philip and Peter, along with some friends. In the 1920s, with funds raised by public subscription, land was bought along Three Bridges Road in memory of those from Crawley who died in the First World War. Sir John Drughorn of Ifield Hall donated gates with plaques commemorating those who died in both world wars, and a drinking water fountain was placed in the Rec in memory of local doctor Timothy Martin (1836-1914). It was not until after the First World War that, in a town surrounded by fields, land was made available for public recreation. In the inter-war years, the Rec lived up to its name by being a recreation ground where cricket matches and school sporting events were held. With the creation of the New Town and recreation grounds in the neighbourhoods, the area was landscaped into the more formal Memorial Gardens. Enjoying a new lease of life since the opening of County Mall, the Memorial Gardens also house wooden benches commemorating local residents. One of the most recent is in memory of my uncle Doug Bastable (seen second from the right in the 1930 snapshot) and his wife Ethel, who died within a few weeks of each other in 2001-2.

Without doubt, the part of Crawley most closely associated with its development as a Victorian New Town has to be Robinson Road, previously New Road, Church Road and Post Office Road. While not purpose-built in the same way as the twentieth-century New Town, Robinson Road nonetheless housed most of the institutions of the Victorian town as can be seen with its various names. When photographed here around a century ago, (top) Robinson Road housed two churches (the Bethel and Congregational chapels), the cottage hospital, the British School and the post office, along with a variety of semi-detached and detached villas. This heyday lasted almost exactly 100 years from the 1850s to the 1950s. For such an elegant and distinguished part of Old Crawley, Robinson Road's decline was so slow and tortuous over a number of years that for some, its final demise in 2002 came almost as a relief. The site where Robinson Road once stood has now been swallowed up in the recent Asda development. For this reason it was quite a challenge to reproduce the old photograph from the same location.

Robinson Road was named in 1928 in honour of Mrs Sarah Robinson, whose fund-raising efforts led to the building of what was originally known as the British School in 1854. At this time elementary education was not compulsory by law and most schools relied on religious organisations such as the British & Foreign Schools Society and the Anglican National Society for the Education of the Poor in the Principles of the Established Church. Mrs Robinson, a Quaker lady from Manor House Farm at County Oak to the north of Crawley, was largely responsible for the founding of the National School in Ifield Road in the 1820s, and thirty years later she felt bound to provide a school for all children, regardless of church attendance. This led to the founding of the British School. This old photograph shows the school with adjoining Headmaster's house as it would have appeared in the late nineteenth century until its demolition and rebuilding in 1916, after which it became known as Crawley Council School. It remained here until 1954, when its pupils were transferred to Crawley New Town schools. For many years after that it became an annexe to Crawley College and was demolished in 1995. The sites of both schools have become absorbed by the High Street relief road and Asda complex, but the new photograph shows the approximate location of the British School today.

moved their large family from London to Vine Cottage at the corner of what was later Robinson Road. The Lemons considered Crawley to be the best of both worlds: a perfect rural setting, whilst easily accessible to Mark's London office by train, making him one of Crawley's first commuters. The first photograph shows Vine Cottage as it was in the 1860s when the family lived there. The same view in 2003 (left) is virtually unrecognisable due to the construction of the Asda superstore, while the only building to be in both photographs is The Morning Star to the right. In the twelve years he lived in Crawley, Mark Lemon plunged himself into local events and entertainments. Among the best known were his regular 'Penny Readings'

No history of Old Crawley would be complete without Mark Lemon (1809-1870) (opposite top) who lived at Vine Cottage from 1858 until his death in May 1870. Friend of Charles Dickens and co-founder of *Punch* magazine from 1841, Mark Lemon and his wife Nellie held at The Station Inn Assembly Rooms – evening concerts made up of amateur theatricals, readings from novels and poetry and musical items. He also patronised the foundation of the Crawley Fire Brigade in 1866. The photograph below shows Crawley Fire Station on the corner of Ifield Avenue at the Northgate end of the High Street. Mark Lemon's memory was revived in June 2000 with the unveiling by Crawley Arts Council and West Sussex County Council of a blue plaque outside The George Hotel, where he held *Punch* editorial meetings. The Penny Readings have also been revived in more modern form with the establishment in 1991 of the Mark Lemon Society, which meets at The George four times a year.

This old photograph dates from the end of the First World War and shows the progress of the urbanisation of Crawley High Street. By this time, virtually all Crawley High Street's private residences at this end of town had been converted to retail premises. The Victorian villas seen in the middle of the photograph on the corner of Three Bridges Road have all been converted to shops, as has the garden of Vine Cottage opposite. From Three Bridges Road and Robinson Road, all this part of the High Street with the exception of part of Vine Cottage was developed after the coming of the railway to Crawley in 1848. The 2003 view shows that hardly any part of it survives. The shops on the corner of Three Bridges Road were demolished in 1958 starting with Wilkins the butchers, while those facing have been demolished over the past ten years, starting with Vine Cottage in 1995 and ending with the remaining few in 2002 for the Asda Superstore development. The construction of the relief road and its semi-pedestrianisation in the 1990s virtually cut off this southern part of Crawley High Street.

This is a close-up view of what once had been Victorian private residences, but were extensively remodelled as shops in 1905. This is testified by the wrought iron-work over what had been Mr Wilkins' butchers shop but which, at the time of this photograph around 1953, was part of Crawley Co-op. By the early 1950s, this small parade of shops was a combination of national retail outlets and local family businesses. A few doors on from the Co-op was the Crawley branch of W.H. Smith & Son Newsagents, Booksellers, Stationers and Diestampers. Two doors further along from this was a branch of one of Crawley High Street's family businesses, tobacconist and hairdresser A.G. Kale. The tall building to the far right was Crawley post office, built in 1928 and severely damaged by air attack in 1943. Following the post office's move to the New Town Centre in 1959, the building became Crawley Library in the early 1960s after which it moved to its current premises in Northgate Avenue. The building was demolished in the 1990s. Today a very distinctive, lantern-topped Providian office block, which has certainly made a major contribution to the modern Crawley skyline, stands on the site.

This was the first view of Crawley for those who travelled to the town by rail in the early 1950s and shows what was still a thriving part of the High Street. It was only with the demolition of the old Crawley railway station and the opening of the new one further along the line in 1968 that this area began its slow decline. This old photograph shows the variety of architecture and retail outlets in Crawley High Street (which was still the town's principle shopping centre even though the New Town was already five years old) better than any other. As the emphasis had firstly been on industry and the neighbourhoods, it was not until the mid to late 1950s that High Street businesses were drawn to the New Town Shopping Centre that developed around Queens Square. Strange to modern eyes is the absence of traffic, road markings, parking restrictions and traffic lights, as it is inconceivable today that cars could just pull up outside a shop. The photograph almost certainly dates from the summer of 1953, since the *Crawley Observer* shop is topped with decorations celebrating the Queen's Coronation. Today only that building (now the Taj Mahal Indian restaurant) and the empty shop opposite (Sadlers the chemists in 1953) survive. The more recent photograph, taken exactly fifty years later in the summer of 2003, shows the development of the Asda superstore which will hopefully inject some life back into this part of Old Crawley.

This old photograph showing the area only a few yards to the right of the previous one dates from around the same time. Taken from the railway signal box, it shows the Station Approach to what fifty years ago was a busy goods yard as well as a passenger station. On the corner of Station Road stood The Cabin, a small newsagency branch of W.H. Smith's and a taxi office. This was one of the locations for the 1954 Norman Wisdom film *One Good Turn*, co-starring Thora Hird. The scene shows Norman somehow losing his trousers on the train to Brighton and being thrown off at Crawley. Wearing just his jacket and baggy underpants he joins a group of walkers and so evades the police. What was around a minute of footage apparently took hours to film, and such a disruptive occasion is unthinkable today! Features long gone but worth mentioning are the large mirror enabling the signal-box keeper (Mr Oliver) to see traffic on the other side of the crossing and the steps to the underpass which allowed pedestrians to pass under the High Street when the railway gates were closed. The 2003 photograph was taken at the foot of the Signal Box, now restored by the Crawley Signal Box Preservation Society. The Station Approach and its small shops have now disappeared under a major road junction, while the underpass was filled in with the installation of the continental railway gates in 1978.

Undoubtedly Old Crawley's smallest shop was The Cabin on Station Approach. Owned by Mrs Braidwood (always known as 'Auntie'), during the late 1950s it was managed by my aunt, Margaret Borrer (née Bastable)

photographed here around 1957 with her assistant, Bunty Kilgower (on the right). Selling tobacco, cigarettes and sweets, Margaret and Bunty did a roaring trade in the 1950s not only from regular commuters, but also from the workmen who travelled to Crawley each day while the New Town was being built. In the days when most adults smoked, the trade in cigarettes and tobacco was a very specialised one and Margaret had to familiarise herself with the various brands, bearing in mind the tastes of her customers. The Cabin, along with Station Approach and the railway station itself, were demolished in 1968. In June 2003, Margaret Borrer stands on the traffic island where The Cabin once stood.

This old photograph of Crawley railway crossing dates from about 1900. Built by the London, Brighton & South Coast Railway Co., the Three Bridges to Horsham branch line, passing through Crawley, was opened in February 1848. The coming of the railway to Crawley was as great a catalyst to change as the New Town was a century later, as it led to development in the area south of the line which became known as Crawley's Victorian New Town. Compared to the same view today, relatively little has changed over the past 100 years, even down to the horse and cart waiting patiently for the train to pass before the gates were opened. Apart from the wooden premises of Fillery & Nightingale to the right and those on the corner of Springfield Road, all the buildings still remain. The signal box, built in 1877, was 'decommissioned' in the 1980s in favour of automation, and has since been restored by the Crawley Signal Box Preservation Society which opens it to the public on a regular basis. To the left is what for many years was The Railway Hotel, although known originally as The Station Inn, and later as both The Rocket and The Firecracker & Firkin. Having been recently re-christened The Railway, the wheel has almost turned full circle.

A longside The Cabin ran quiet and leafy Station Road, comprising detached and semi-detached villas, and the Crawley Baptist Chapel seen here in the old photograph during the 1900s. Crawley's Baptist congregation first met at the Temperance Reading Room on Crawley Green from where they resolved to found their own, permanent place of worship. The first non-conformist place of worship to be built in the centre of Crawley was the Reformed Baptist Chapel in 1858, followed by the Congregational Chapel some time afterwards. Both were situated in Robinson Road, then more appropriately known as Church Road. The Baptist Chapel's founding minister when its Station Road premises were built in 1883 was the Revd James McAuslane, a student of the great Baptist preacher Revd C.H. Spurgeon. Until he left Crawley in 1909, Mr McAuslane was very much involved in local life on issues involving politics, social reform and temperance and was a member of Crawley Parish Council, the Board of Guardians, the Board of Governors of one of Crawley's schools and the management committee of the

Crawley and Ifield Co-operative Society. Sadly, the Baptist Chapel was severely damaged in the 1943 air raid, its surviving part becoming Crawley Library in the 1950s and more recently Crawley Boxing Club. The 2003 photograph of what is now Station Way shows the site of the Crawley Baptist Chapel now occupied by a multi-storey car park. During the second half of the nineteenth century and the years leading up to the First World War, concerns about the effects of alcohol on family life were strong and the Temperance movement gained a lot of support. The photograph below shows the banner of the Crawley Temperance Society being held among the throng of people marching from the railway station to The Square for a memorial service for Edward VII in May 1910. The last photograph, taken in June 2003, shows the partially completed Crawley Baptist Church in Crabtree Road.

Crawley railway station's station master and staff photographed in a quiet moment just over a century ago. The station stood here for 120 years, from 1848 until its demolition in 1968. This is the view from the Three Bridges-bound platform which led to the London to Brighton main line, the opening of which in 1841 virtually killed off Crawley's coaching trade. For most of the 1840s Crawley was a rural backwater with the nearby village of Three Bridges set to supersede it. The London, Brighton & South Coast Railway Co. considered two options for the proposed branch line from Three Bridges to Horsham: one was to run north of Tilgate Forest, while the other was to run south. Fortunately for Crawley the former was chosen, restoring the town's fortunes and leading to considerable expansion. *Punch* editor Mark Lemon, one of Crawley's first commuters during the 1860s, could get to London in just

over an hour. To the left, behind the Horsham-bound platform, stood the original Station Inn Assembly Rooms, where Lemon and his family produced the popular Penny Readings. The Assembly Rooms became a central part of Crawley's social life over the next 100 years, most notably during the Second World War when Mrs Longley's Accordion Band regularly entertained troops on leave with their girlfriends. The Assembly Rooms were destroyed by fire in 1966. As well as operating a thriving passenger service, Crawley also had its own goods yard and depot, as seen in the photograph (opposite top) from around 1958. A lot of merchandise arrived by rail, such as my grandfather's daily delivery of fish in wooden crates which in the 1950s and '60s my uncle Philip Bastable would wheel down the High Street to their shop in The Square. The same view in 2003 shows the extent of dereliction of the area today.

Technically, Crawley High Street ended at the railway crossing, the other side of which was Brighton Road, but the journey from The Sun to The Half Moon did not end here. This old photograph from the late 1890s shows the other side of the railway crossing, looking in the opposite direction to that shown on p.55. Although the 2003 photograph shows the buildings to the right still remaining, the balcony on the first floor of The Railway Hotel from where public announcements such as General Election results were made has long since disappeared. Many years later, the first floor over Skinner's the bakers became the Cutty Sark coffee bar, where, at the age of eight I was taken one evening by my aunt, Margaret, as a treat. In the corner stood a juke box which, fed with sixpences, played current hits such as 'Claudette' by the Everly Brothers and 'Stupid Cupid' by Connie Francis. The opposite side of the road is now entirely changed, with the wooden premises of Fillery & Nightingale – corn and coal merchants replaced by the castellated London & County Bank in 1902, later Lloyds Bank and today Brace & Oakley estate agency. Apart from the new bank premises, the field alongside was soon occupied by Mr Gadsdon's motor garage. As well as his garage, Mr Gadsdon also built Crawley's first permanent cinema, The Imperial Picture Theatre, in 1911. Coincidentally, it was destroyed by fire in 1928 – the same year in which the 'talkies' first hit the silver screen.

The rebuilding in 1928 of what was then known as the Imperial Cinema opened a new era for popular entertainment in Crawley, with the Imperial being the town's only cinema for ten years before the opening of the Embassy in 1938. As well as offering an hour or more of entertainment from the Hollywood 'dream factory', the Imperial was also the venue for the more serious issues which increasingly confronted the 1930s. One such occasion was the addressing of a League of Nations Association meeting by Prime Minister Ramsay MacDonald. The Imperial became no match for the more modern and plush Embassy down the road, and the building was re-deployed firstly as an auction room and then taken over by Gadsdons as a car showroom. Despite the modern ground-floor facilities it has today, the distinctive features of the Imperial Cinema, such as its name and date, remain literally set in stone.

At the Imperial Cinema, Crawley's shops rapidly gave way to the large villas which characterised Brighton Road. These houses were occupied at the end of the nineteenth and beginning of the twentieth centuries by local professional men and their families. One such man was Moses Nightingale of Fillery & Nightingale – corn and coal merchants.

Moses Nightingale and his wife Ruth lived with their family at Hazeldene on Brighton Road, which was built in 1896. Apart from the business side of his life, Moses Nightingale is remembered for the Hazeldene Orchestra founded by him and his wife in 1884. Like the Rector of Crawley and the Longleys of The Beeches of East Park, Moses and Ruth Nightingale would occasionally open their gardens for fêtes or dancing displays. One such occasion was a celebration of Queen Victoria's Diamond Jubilee in 1897, with children dressed as national figures such as Britannia (to the left). Following the deaths in the 1930s of Moses and Ruth Nightingale (whose gravestone in St John's churchyard includes sheaves of corn), Hazeldene remained within the family until the late 1960s when it became the premises of the Crawley Club.

No history of Old or New Crawley can be written or compiled without reference to the Longley construction company and in particular Sir Norman Longley (1900–94). The firm of Sir Norman's grandfather James Longley moved to Crawley from Turners Hill in 1881and took over a site alongside the railway line previously owned by Sumners the brick makers. Over the next few years, Longleys grew around its Steam Joinery Works at the end of East Park, seen here under construction in the 1880s. As well as the company works, James Longley built what amounted to a small township for its workforce in East Park and Malthouse Road within a short distance of his own house 'The Beeches'. As building contractors, Longleys were not only responsible for the construction of housing in Southgate on Brighton Road, Goffs Park Road, East Park and Malthouse Road, but also a number of prestigious projects such as Christ's Hospital School near Horsham and Lancing College Chapel. Longleys also enjoyed a reputation for specialist skills and were responsible for the restoration of Westminster Abbey choir stalls after the Second World War. The firm went on to became very much involved with the building of Crawley New Town and the quality of their craftsmanship was matched by Norman Longley's involvement in so many aspects of local life. Knighted in 1966 for his services to the British construction industry, Norman Longley was equally committed to both Old and New Crawley. The 2003 photograph shows a large hotel now standing on the site of Longleys Steam Joinery Works.

The Brighton Road heading out of Crawley was part of the original London to Brighton road which had set the town on the map in the eighteenth and early nineteenth centuries. Unlike the North toll gate, which is easy to plot, the actual location of the South toll gate from which this part of Old and New Crawley gets its name is not clear. It is thought to have stood at the foot of Hoggs Hill looking north back into Crawley. At this time, Brighton Road was lined by the villas of local professionals such as Moses Nightingale and Dr Timothy Martin, many of which were constructed by Longleys. Although many have since been demolished and replaced by modern blocks of flats, Brighton Road still has a leafy, residential air about it. At the likely location of the South toll gate the road rose at Hoggs Hill, with Hoggs Hill Farm where Southgate West First and Middle School now stand, and Hill Top Farm on the current site of Southgate First and Middle School. On the crest of Hoggs Hill stood The Half Moon public house, built by another of Victorian Crawley's builders, Richard Cook, whose yard was at the top of what is now Perryfield Road. The Half Moon is as popular today as it was a century ago.

A lmost certainly the most significant and far reaching event in Crawley's long history was its designation in January 1947 as one of post-war Britain's 'Mark 1' New Towns. Along with Stevenage, Harlow, Hemel Hempstead, Hatfield, Basildon, Welwyn Garden City and Bracknell, Crawley was to be planned and developed as a showpiece town by a Development Corporation appointed by the government, or more specifically, Labour's Minister of Town and Country Planning, Lewis Silkin. From its base at Broadfield, an eighteenth-century house from which one of Crawley New Town's neighbourhoods was later to derive its name, the Development Corporation's team of planners, architects and engineers, led by Sir Thomas Bennett, set about planning the perfect town. One of the first outcomes was the unveiling of planning consultant Anthony Minoprio's Crawley New Town Master Plan in December 1948. Inspired to a very great extent by Ebenezer Howard's Garden City Movement, Minoprio's Master Plan was set out in zones for industry, the town centre and above all the neighbourhoods, each with its school, church, parade of shops and variety of housing. In dramatic contrast to Old Crawley and the High Street in particular, New Crawley as represented here was planned to the finest detail, with a projected population of 50,000 by 1963 when the project was supposed to be completed. Although highly trained professionals, the New Town planners could not have foreseen that once development had started, it became virtually impossible to draw a halt. Forty years on from the magic 'cut off' point, Crawley's population is double its 1948

Chapter 2

NEW CRAWLEY

prediction, and given the likely development of Gatwick Airport (which played no part in the 1948 Master Plan) and the general economic prosperity of the area, there is no sign of slowing up. In following the 'Then & Now' format, the second section of the book will focus on the extent to which the precise plans and predictions of over fifty years ago have been realised.

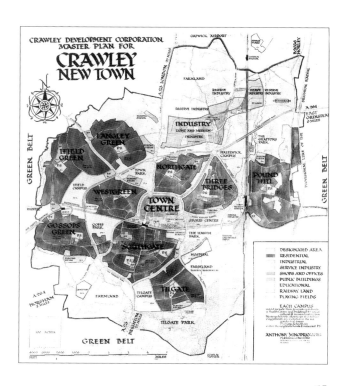

PRINCESS ELIZABETH
AND
THE NEW CRAWLEY

"COURIER" SOUVENIR OF THE ROYAL VISIT

had been no official visit to Crawley by a leading member of the Royal Family until Princess Elizabeth came to inaugurate Crawley New Town and open the Industrial Area on 25 January 1950. The photograph above shows Princess Elizabeth cutting the ribbon in front of a choir, giving the occasion a spiritual as well as a political and social dimension. It was significant that Princess Elizabeth inaugurated not just Crawley, but the whole post-war New Town movement at the undeveloped Industrial Area. The image on the left is taken from the cover of a souvenir of the occasion published by the *Crawley Courier*. The young newly-married Princess represented the hopes and aspirations of a new age just as Diana, Princess of Wales would a generation later. When she became Queen Elizabeth II two years later, the national media went to town proclaiming a 'new Elizabethan age'. If the second Queen Elizabeth was to be personally identified with the hopes and aspirations of New Britain, so over the next ten years was New Crawley.

Other than the Prince Regent regularly passing through en route to his Pavilion at Brighton and the (almost certainly mythical) visit of Queen Elizabeth I, there

One of the over-riding principles of Ebenezer Howard's 1898 *Garden City* was that the worst aspects of the Industrial Revolution be remedied by re-locating industry away from 'the smoke' (which in Crawley's case was south London) and into the country. This principle was adopted by the 1946 Act of Parliament which conceived Crawley and its fellow New Towns, and industrial relocation was the first practical step to be taken. Consequently land was set aside to the north of the town to develop light industry in spacious, rural surroundings away from residential areas. Previously known by its working title of Crawley Factory Estate, this land was christened by the Princess as Manor Royal after nearby Manor House Farm, home of

nineteenth-century philanthropist Mrs Sarah Robinson. It is difficult to grasp that what today is a grassy island on Manor Royal's very busy road junction marks a major turning point not just in Crawley's, but in Britain's history.

This view of Crawley New Town's Manor Royal Industrial Estate from the early 1950s would have been a dream come true for Ebenezer Howard had he lived to see it (he died aged seventy-eight in 1928). This view of Youngmans factory which produced aluminium ladders, with sweet manufacturers Sun d'Or directly opposite, represented an ideal in town-planning quite unique at the time. Youngmans and Sun d'Or have long since gone, but the 2003 view of the Manor Royal Industrial Estate (left) with its trees and grassy banks re-emphasises that the Garden City dream of a century ago continues to be realised through the marriage of the industrial with the rural.

Despite Youngmans' prestigious location on Manor Royal, the industrial estate's major stakeholder was the Aluminium Plant Vessel Company (APV) (below) which moved to Crawley from London when its Chairman, Dr Richard Seligman laid the works' foundation stone in November 1951. Like Youngmans and other companies which moved to Crawley New Town, A.P.V. saw itself and its workforce as pioneers, not just within the workplace, but also within the overall development of Crawley New Town. Once a shining example of both the Garden City and New Town movements, the APV site was demolished in the 1980s and is now occupied by Crawley Business Park (left).

One of only a few of Manor Royal's original buildings to survive is what in 1953 was the premises of Lloyds Register of Shipping. Considerably smaller than Youngmans, APV and Manor Royal's other giants, the Lloyds building is a classic example of 1950s design at its best. Although adapted over time, this building's simple architectural lines do not date fifty years on. The saplings of 1953 have grown into sturdy trees and continue to make Ebenezer Howard's and the early New Town planners' dreams a reality in 2003.

It was never the intention of its architects and planners that Crawley New Town should be classless, but rather that all classes and age groups should live alongside each other in the same neighbourhood. In the early days, the Development Corporation's professionals and managerial white-collar workers lived only doors away from those who worked on the shop floor. West Green was very much the flagship neighbourhood, with its wide grass verges, open greens and the variety of housing seen in this 1950s photograph (below). Distinctive features of West Green neighbourhood's housing included the groups of pink-washed 'Star' flats, so-called because of their three-sided design, and the larger semi-detached and detached houses unsubsidised to attract higher income families thus ensuring a social balance. Over fifty years on, West Green's houses, bungalows and flats have changed remarkably little. The main differences, yet again, are the vast increase in trees and shrubbery and the fact that many residents have since bought their properties and carried out their own alterations.

Central as it was to the Garden City and New Town ideal, the relocation of industry from south London to Crawley was only part of the grand scheme. Parallel to the planning and building of modern factories and offices within a rural environment was the creation of well-equipped housing for their workforce. Crawley New Town's houses, flats and bungalows were built to the neighbourhood pattern, which despite its modern architecture was planned to emulate traditional self-contained villages each with its own shops, school, church, local public house and community centre. Having named the Manor Royal Estate during her January 1950 visit, Princess Elizabeth went on to pay a call at a house in Smalls Mead, the first road in Crawley New Town's first neighbourhood West Green. It was around this time that south London companies moving to Crawley laid on coaches to introduce their workforce to their new homes. These photographs show two such visits at around that time, the first made in West Green Drive and the second in nearby Buckmans Road. Although the women especially look suitably impressed, moving into a new house in a new neighbourhood in a new town was not without its problems, and 'new town blues' were not unknown. Today, West Green Drive and Buckmans Road have become established parts of the town with some of the original new town pioneers still living in the houses they moved into over fifty years ago.

school played a vital part in this community-building process, as did the development of the neighbourhood Community Associations. Thanks to three men – Norman Longley, Albert Weston and Harry Frost – each neighbourhood was provided with a Community hut, usually close to the parade of shops and where morning, afternoon and evening social events would take place. The first, West Green Community Association, moved from its hut to brick premises adjoining West Green School in 1954. The old photograph shows a talk being given in one of the Community Association Huts in the early 1950s, while the second shows the West Green Community Association building from the perspective of the Green, still rural today.

There were many who realised that creating a New Town was not just about planning roads and designing and building fine houses and schools, but also about bringing people together and forging the sort of community they had left behind them. The neighbourhood

The most impressive part of Crawley New Town is The New Town Shopping Centre, which offers the most striking contrast with the Old, since it adjoins the High Street, where this compilation both begins and ends. Detailed plans drawn up in the late 1940s showed a Town Centre which was to be developed in different stages and focused on a central piazza. Photographs of the architect's model and an aerial view from about 1957 highlight this contrast, for whereas Crawley High Street developed over centuries to no plan, with buildings dating back nearly eight hundred years, Crawley's New Town Centre was to be designed, laid out and built within less than ten years. The first stage to be built was The Broadwalk which opened out into the High Street.

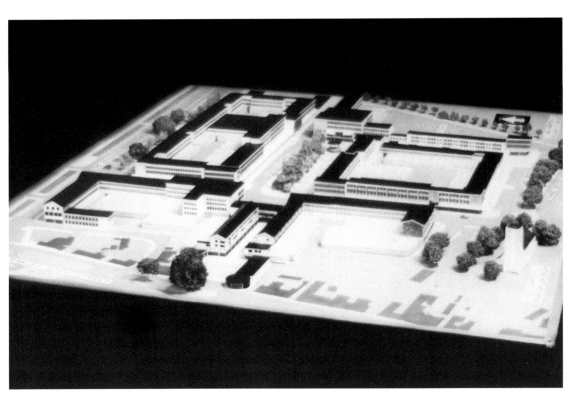

If the building of factories and housing was the Crawley Development Corporation's primary concern, the provision of schools came a close second as most New Town pioneers had small children. Just as West Green was the New Town's first neighbourhood, so West Green School was its first school. Comprising of both Infant and Junior sections, West Green School was under the headship of Mr Dennis (Juniors) and Mrs Howse (Infants). As with housing, West Green School was something of a flagship, both in design and in the realisation of West Sussex County Council that neighbourhood schools were to play an essential part in community-building. Although the buildings still stand, social changes over the past fifty years are shown by the fact that what once was the Junior School is now part of an Adult Education Centre, while a large section of the playing fields alongside the modern West Green First School has been made over to the building of flats and bungalows for the elderly.

Following on from the building of homes and schools, the next priority for Crawley New Town was the Neighbourhood Centre. An essential part of each of the Crawley New Town Neighbourhood Centres was the public house. Victorian suspicions of alcohol and the dubious reputation of public houses had all but disappeared by the early 1950s. The Development Corporation and breweries regarded the public house as an important part of community and family life and certainly not the sole prerogative of men. It was assumed that they would be joined at the bar by their wives, and most neighbourhood pubs provided a children's room or garden. Many of Crawley New Town's neighbourhood public houses were given historic names with local associations, such as Northgate's Black Dog (shown in the first photograph) named after the old Black Dog Lane nearby. The Neighbourhood Centre also included a parade of shops. Not only did the planners foresee each neighbourhood as a self-contained 'township', but they correctly assumed that most women would be housewives and mothers who would rely on the shops for their daily needs. Therefore, each neighbourhood shopping parade would have its traditional grocer, greengrocer, chemist, newsagent, sweet shop and tobacconist. Today, Northgate's public house (opposite below) and its shops (right) look much the same, although in common with virtually all Crawley's Neighbourhood Centres, the shops tend to be more leisure orientated while pub clientele leans more towards the local youth. The final photograph is of the sign announcing the construction of Northgate Neighbourhood Centre.

As each of the New Town neighbourhoods were intended to follow a 'village' pattern, another important element was the Anglican church. As West Green already had St Peter's Church (built in 1892) and Northgate's St Elizabeth's was not opened until 1965 (services having previously been held in a hut), Crawley New Town's first neighbourhood church was St Richard's in the neighbourhood of Three Bridges. One of Crawley New Town's pioneer churches was St Paul's Methodist Church in Northgate, opened in 1953. Although there had been a church in old Three Bridges High Street dedicated to St Richard in the 1930s, it was considered far too small for the greatly expanded area's needs. Designed by church architect N.F. Cachemaille-Day, the new St Richard's was consecrated by Bishop George Bell of Chichester in 1954 (above). With its great height and white stone cross, St Richard's was to become a distinctive part of the Crawley skyline for almost forty years, and was thought of by some as a possible successor to St John's as Crawley's new civic church. Although nothing came of this idea, St Richard's played a very important part in cementing the new community as well as being a place of worship. With the emergence of serious structural faults in the early 1990s, St Richard's was demolished and the land re-deployed for housing and a new smaller church which was consecrated in 1995 by Bishop Lindsay Urwin of Horsham.

As they had for Old Crawley, the Anglican and Roman Catholic Churches played a significant part in the provision of church primary schools in Crawley New Town. One of the first to be built was St Margaret's Church of England Primary School in Ifield, to which Headmaster Mr Albert Weston, staff and children moved from the old West Green Church of England School in April 1955. In contrast to its Victorian predecessor's high-vaulted roofs and tall ecclesiastical-style windows, St Margaret's School was modern, light and airy with a hall which also acted as a chapel. Photographed today, St Margaret's School remains very popular with parents and pupils alike and has been greatly extended to take into account not just rising numbers, but also the demands of the National Curriculum. Despite its obvious architectural advantages, St Margaret's greatest contribution to the development of the New Town was the mixing of children from Old and New Crawley families. Occasions like the annual St Margaret's School sports day seen here in 1961(opposite top) were good examples of the social mixing which was going on in all the neighbourhood schools. This photograph represents the balance of the old with the new – myself, from an Old Crawley family (far left) alongside my friend Kenneth King, whose family moved to Crawley New Town in 1956. The final photograph shows a number of us returning to our old classroom for the retirement party of our much-loved teacher, Joan Witherington almost a quarter of a century later in 1984.

As well as the neighbourhood primary schools, West Sussex County Council also made provision in Crawley New Town for secondary education. As well as the great changes brought to Crawley by its New Town designation, the building of secondary schools in particular was subject to the terms of the 1944 Education Act. This set up the tri-partite system of grammar, technical and modern schools, entry to which was determined by the selective Eleven Plus examination. Crawley New Town's first secondary school was Hazelwick School in Three Bridges. Having left St Margaret's School in 1962 I joined Ifield Grammar, which had been founded alongside the Sarah Robinson Secondary Modern School in 1955. Ifield Grammar was a blend of the new with the traditional, with modern buildings and facilities but with many staff still wearing academic gowns. The apparently unaltered view today reveals few of the changes made to the school, the first of which was its amalgamation with the Sarah Robinson School in 1966 to create Ifield Comprehensive. Now part of Ifield Community College, the 1950s buildings are to be replaced by more modern premises on the same site. Although Ifield Grammar School was effectively eliminated, its past students have remained in touch at several events such as the school hall reunion in April 1993, including founding Headmaster Geoffrey Avery, his successor David Henschel and Deputy Head Margery Lee.

The Anglican and Roman Catholic Churches also made provision for secondary education in Crawley New Town, as they had done with the primary schools of St Margaret's, St Andrew's, St Francis' and Our Lady Queen of Heaven. The first church secondary school was St Wilfrid's Roman Catholic School which was opened in 1953 and the second was The Holy Trinity Church of England School, in the Gossops Green Neighbourhood, in 1967. By that time, all Crawley New Town's secondary schools had become comprehensive, the earliest and most prominent being Thomas Bennett School in Tilgate, named after the first chairman of the Crawley Development Corporation. Like Ifield Grammar, Holy Trinity has enjoyed a mixture of the new with the traditional. Named after the Cathedral Church of the Holy Trinity at Chichester, stones from the cathedral were set in the school's foundation to emphasise its diocesan roots. Early photographs show the school being built around the traditional house system within which an enclosed area (Beith Court) was laid out, with modern photographs showing the same views today. As with St Margaret's, Holy Trinity has remained a much sought after school, with plans for further expansion.

These two photographs show The Broadwalk at different stages of development, using the High Street's Grand Parade and Woolworths as markers to show that each was taken from the same spot. The first dates from not long after The Broadwalk's official opening in 1954 and shows a traffic-free shopping area – considered quite an innovation at the time. Yet despite its modern architecture, The Broadwalk's shops were still of the traditional sort, with the butcher, fishmonger and mini-supermarket each with their shop blinds, the like of which had been seen in the High Street for years. Two of The Broadwalk's most patronised shops in the New Town's early days were Hills & Oliver, which sold paints and wallpaper, and Newtown Baby Needs. The photograph of the Queen walking along The Broadwalk into Crawley High Street with Development Corporation Chairman Sir Thomas Bennett in June 1958 is the frontispiece of this book. The general view of The Broadwalk today shows few changes, although the nature of the shops have changed a good deal and while the flourishing Jubilee Oak has all but obliterated Grand Parade from view.

During its construction in the summer of 1953, The Broadwalk aroused great local interest as the first part of Crawley New Town to make an impact on the old High Street. Particular attention was focused on what became known as the 'round shop' (to the left of the old photograph), which started its life as Jean Bailey's ladies' dress shop and which today is a bookmaker's. The front of The Broadwalk, once occupied by the tiny cottages pictured in the Old Crawley section, was opened up to form the Well, an area for dancing displays, meetings or just enjoying a quiet pint. The Well was re-landscaped a few years ago and its seats have become a popular place for relaxation, especially in the summer. The Jubilee Oak dominates this end of The Broadwalk as it does the High Street. In the 1953 photograph the shops of the Grand Parade can be made out, such as Boots the chemist and

Bellman's, a shop which sold knitting wool, baby clothes and ladies' underwear. Begun in the 1930s, Grand Parade remained only partially finished at the outbreak of war in 1939, and was not completed until 1953/4 when The Broadwalk was being built. A number of Grand Parade shops, including Boots, Bellman's, Tesco and Woolworths, moved to Queens Square in the late 1950s.

The old photograph dates from around 1947 and shows a school teacher carrying out a survey on Crawley with a group of boys, a couple of which appear in the first part of this compilation. A fascinating snapshot, it is one of only a few showing what this part of the town was like before the Town Centre was built in the 1950s. The only clue as to where it might be is the tower of St John's Church to the far left. This area was soon to be developed as The Broadway which, as its name suggests, is a wide thoroughfare between The Broadwalk and Queens Square. The 2003 photograph is taken from approximately the same spot, but only the east end of St John's can now be seen.

This postcard of about 1960 (below) shows Queens Square looking west, with Crawley New Town department store, the Co-op to the right. Moving to its new premises from scattered shops in the High Street in 1957, the Co-op lacked the 1960s glamour and 'fizz' of Queensway Store and for years seemed locked in a pre-war, utilitarian time warp. This changed when its name was altered to Living in the 1980s, which brought a new refit and image that was in tune at last with its time. Since the departure of Living in the 1990s the premises has been occupied by T&G Hughes. One very distinctive feature of what many still regard as the Co-op is the sculpture named 'The Family' on the store's façade which was unveiled by ballerina Dame Alicia Markova in about 1961. Two other artistic features of Queens Square seen here are 'The Boy and the Dolphin' sculpture in the fountain, and the bandstand.

FOUNTAIN AND BANDSTAND, CRAWLEY. L 8105

In much the same way as the High Street was the focus of Old Crawley, so Queens Square became the centre of the New. Named after the Queen, who made her second visit to Crawley New Town in June 1958, Queens Square was laid out from the mid-1950s in the 'piazza' style favoured by architects and town planners not only in the construction of the New Towns, but also in the re-building of Britain's war-ravaged cities. Queens Square was fringed with small shops and large national chain stores such as Sainsbury's, Boots, Timothy Whites, Woolworths and Littlewoods. However, if one shop summed up the new mood of Harold Macmillan's 1950s 'you've never had it so good' Britain it was Queensway Store, which dominated the eastern end of Queens Square. Designed in what then was considered a very modern style, Queensway was the sort of department store only previously found in Brighton, Croydon or London. Its

1960 advertising slogan clearly identified it with Crawley New Town, and declared itself 'a great new store in a great new town'. Not for the first time, the 2003 view has been greatly obscured by trees, two of which were planted by the Queen and Prince Philip during their June 1958 visit. The Queensway Store premises were taken over by Tesco in 1968, and from the late 1980s have been divided up into a number of retail units. The second pair of photographs shows Littlewoods on Queensway, one of the few chain stores to have stayed at the same premises.

The Queens Square bandstand was re-assembled in the 1950s from its original location at Gatwick Racecourse on the site of the present airport. Fortunately, its Edwardian wrought ironwork immediately blended in with Queens Square's 1950s contemporary surroundings. Of the countless performances it has staged over the last forty or more years, among the most memorable were the Sunday afternoon 'trad jazz' sessions of the early 1960s. Crawley New Town's youth would jive to the live music of the New City Jazzmen and clarinettist Acker Bilk who hit the charts in 1961 with his haunting 'Stranger on the Shore'. With the re-landscaping of Queens Square in the 1990s, the bandstand was renovated and moved to its present location, while 'The Boy and the Dolphin' sculpture now stands in the less vulnerable surroundings of Crawley Borough Council's Town Hall.

What, at the time of this photograph in about 1960 was one of the town centre's more obscure offshoots, The Martletts has since become one of its main thoroughfares with the building of County Mall in the early 1990s. In 1960 The Martletts led to the bus station and pointed out of Crawley, while in 2003 it leads the shopper further into the town. Shopping malls have become one of the main retail revolutions of the last ten years, with County Mall marking Crawley not as New or Old, but as a regional centre growing from where it began nearly 800 years ago as *crow lea* – the forest clearing with crows. Whether Old or New, Crawley has never stood still, and even as this book goes to press, plans are

surging ahead for further development at Gatwick Airport and in the town centre, launching the town into the first decade of the twenty-first century.

Her Majesty the Queen paid a third visit to Crawley New Town in December 1969 when she officially opened Holy Trinity school. She is seen here with founding Headmaster Robert Snell and departmental head Gillian Penny inspecting the new Home Economics rooms. Teaching at Holy Trinity myself since 1973 has enabled me to see the onset, not only of the twenty-first century, but also of Crawley New Town's third and fourth generations.

About the Author

Roger Bastable was born in October 1950, a few months after Princess Elizabeth formally inaugurated Crawley New Town and opened the Manor Royal Industrial Estate. Born into a High Street trading family, Roger grew up as both an Old and a New Towner. From 1955 he attended St Margaret's Church of England Primary School and went on in 1962 to what was then Ifield Grammar School. Roger has spent only four years away from Crawley, from 1969 to 1972 when he studied History at the University of Newcastle Upon Tyne and from 1972 to 1973 when he took his postgraduate Certificate in Education at Christ Church College, Canterbury. Since 1973 he has been on the staff at the Holy Trinity Church of England Comprehensive School in Gossops Green, where he is now teaching the children of his original students. Roger became actively involved in the history of Crawley in 1980 and this is his fourth book about the town. Over the last twenty-three years he has lectured and broadcast on Crawley's history, was Chairman of the Crawley Museum Society and writes regularly for the local press. He was a co-founder of the Crawley Festival in 1985 and Churchwarden of St John's Church from 1986 to 2002. Roger is currently working on a D.Phil. thesis on Crawley New Town at the University of Sussex.